BRAIN GA

MW00955233

Get Ready for
PRESCHOOL

·······

Picture Puzzles
for Growing Minds

pil

Publications International, Ltd.

What is STEM?

The acronym STEM stands for Science, Technology, Engineering, and Math. STEM is not just about knowledge, but also about how to obtain, process, and apply that knowledge. The skills involved include observation, investigation, understanding, and problem-solving. Introducing these concepts early on can help foster children's curiosity and build the skills they need to understand the world around them.

Play to LEARN.

The picture puzzles in this book encourage children to explore and learn, even as they play! Sometimes puzzlers are encouraged to look closely at a picture for details, or to take a wider view to plan their path through a maze. At other times, they can try out their logic skills to solve the puzzle. Throughout the book, bright, colorful pictures and challenging games keep children interested and entertained.

The puzzles may be done in any order, and with or without help from an adult. Kids can use the table of contents to find their favorite types of puzzles, or dive straight in!

Contents

Contents

Follow Me

Draw the path that goes through every cactus.

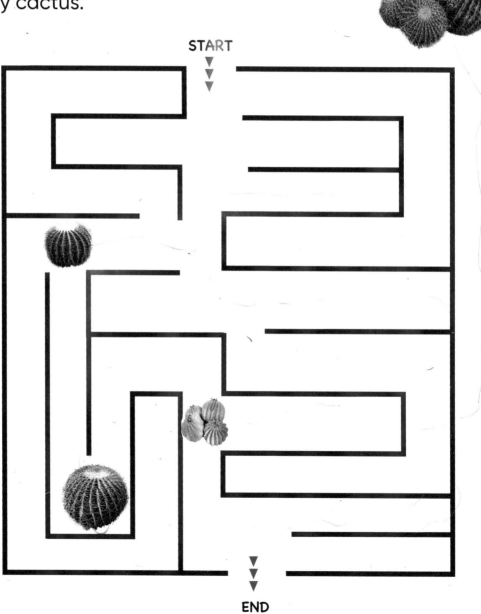

START

END

Answers on page 106.

Step by Step

Follow each step to get to the last robot.

1	START	
2	GO ▶ 4 spots to	
3	GO ▼ 2 spots to	
4	GO ◀ 1 spot to	

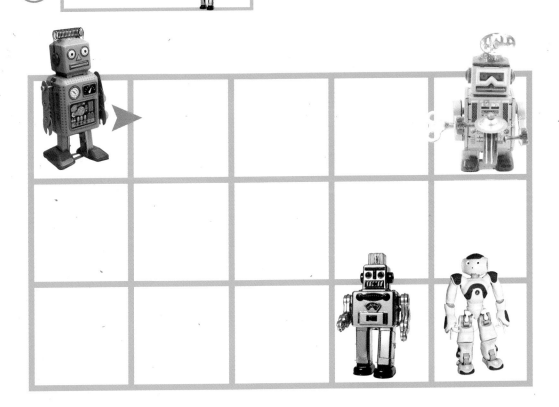

Match It

Draw a line to connect each worker to the matching tool.

Answers on page 106.

Spot the Shape

Find the triangle inside the photo.

Odd One Out

Circle the object that does not belong.

Answers on page 107.

Do It!

Drop this book! Then turn this page.

What Happened?

Answers on page 107.

Point

Point to the raccoon's:

- Ears
- Nose
- Tail
- Paws

What Is Next?

What comes next in each pattern?

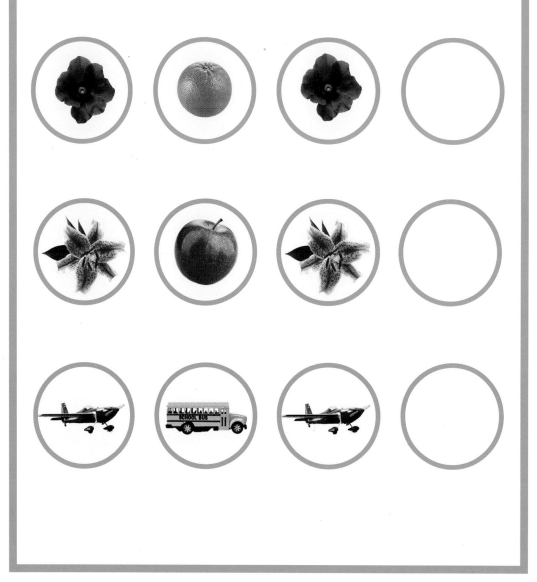

Answers on page 107.

Zoom In

Which fruit matches the big picture?

Two by Two

Draw a line to connect each beaker with its twin.

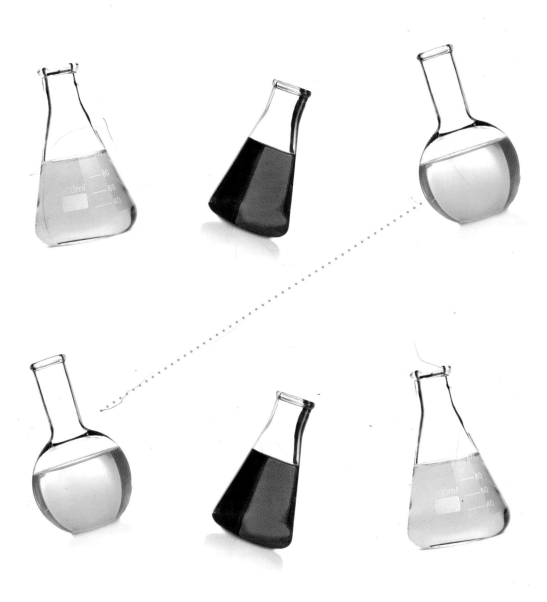

Answers on page 108.

Find It

Circle these 3 fish in the picture.

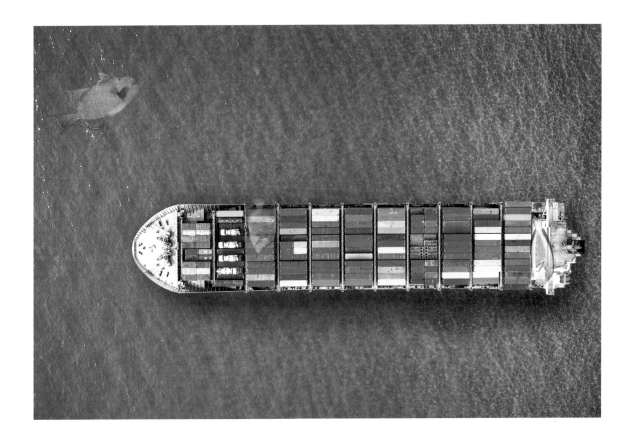

What Fits?

Which of these things would you use in cold weather?

Answers on page 108.

Draw It

Draw the missing parts.

- Draw 2 wheels

- Draw 1 seat

What Is Different?

Circle 2 differences between these pictures.

Answers on page 109.

Out of Order

These images are in the wrong order! What is the right order?

Hide and Seek

Can you find the banana hiding among the tools?

Answers on page 109.

Memory

Look at this picture for 1 minute. Remember it!
Then turn the page.

What is different here? Find 1 thing that is different.

Answers on page 110.

Follow Me

Draw the path that goes through every brick.

START

END

Step by Step

Follow each step to get to the potted plant.

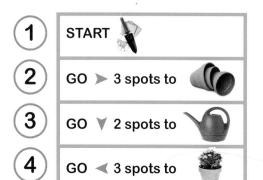

1. START
2. GO ▶ 3 spots to
3. GO ▼ 2 spots to
4. GO ◀ 3 spots to

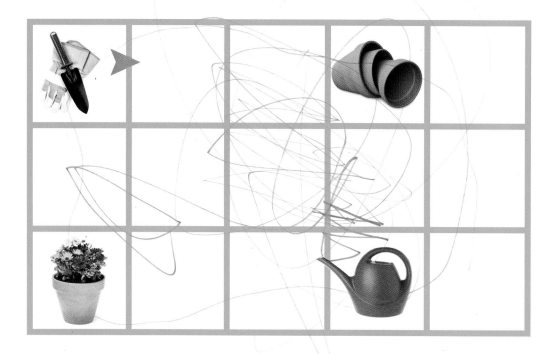

26

Answers on page 110.

Match It

Draw a line to connect each pair of similar animals.

Answers on page 110.

Spot the Shape

Find the triangle inside the photo.

Answers on page 111.

Odd One Out

Circle the animal that does not belong.

Point

Point to the tree's:

- Leaves
- Branches
- Trunk

Answers on page 111.

Do It!

Turn this book upside down! Then turn the page.

What happened?

Answers on page 111.

What Is Next?

What comes next in each pattern?

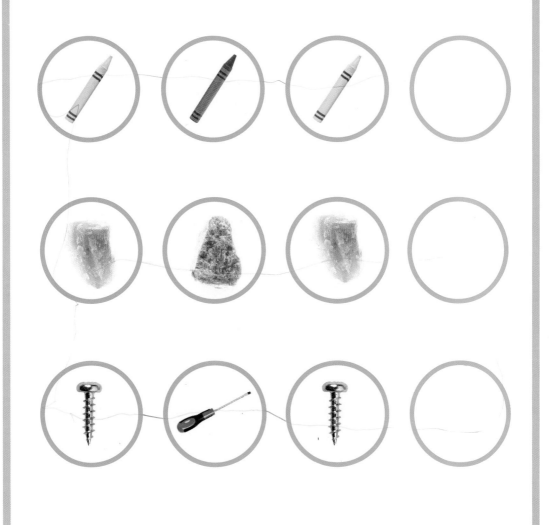

Zoom In

Which animal matches the big picture?

34

Answers on page 112.

Two by Two

Draw a line to connect each coat with its twin.

Find It

Circle these 3 tools in the picture.

Answers on page 112.

What Fits?

Which of these animals are birds?

Draw It

Draw the missing parts.

- Draw 2 wheels

- Draw 1 truck bed

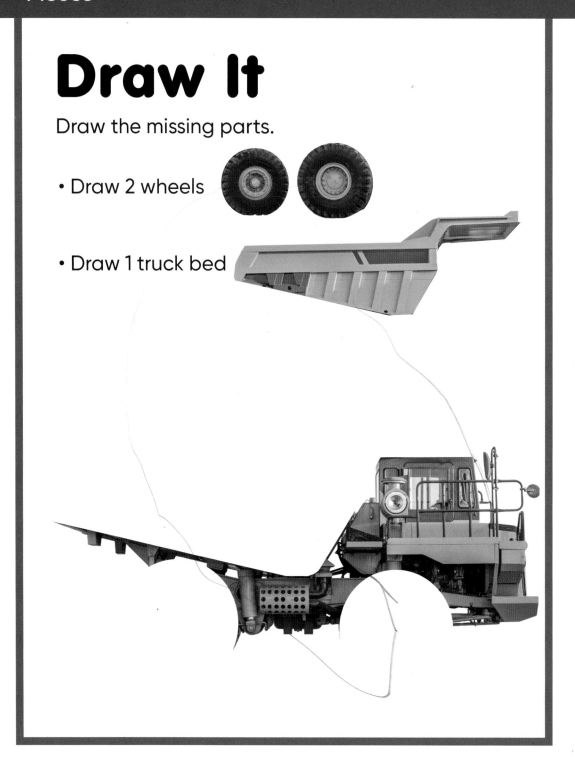

Answers on page 113.

What Is Different?

Circle the 3 differences between these pictures.

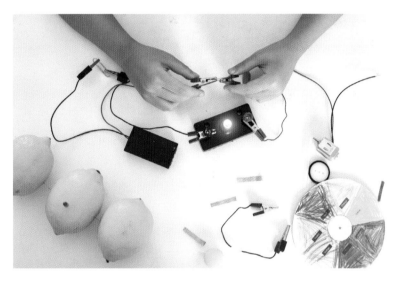

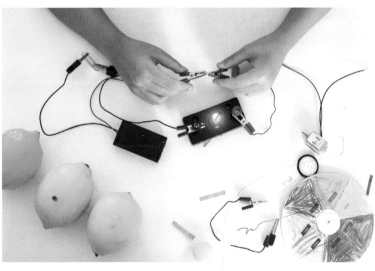

Out of Order

These images are in the wrong order! What is the right order?

Answers on page 113.

Memory

Look at this picture for 1 minute. Remember it!
Then turn the page.

What is different here? Find 3 things that are different.

Answers on page 114.

Hide and Seek

Circle the block hiding among the vegetables.

Follow Me

Draw the path that goes through every robot part.

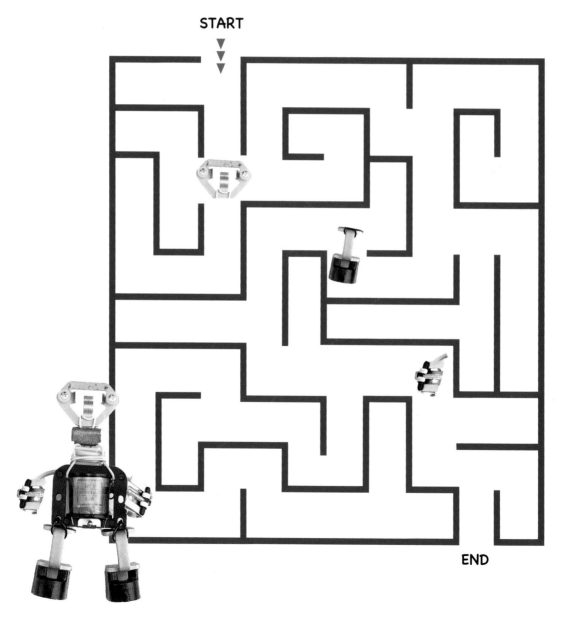

START

END

Answers on page 114.

Step by Step

Follow each step to travel to every planet.

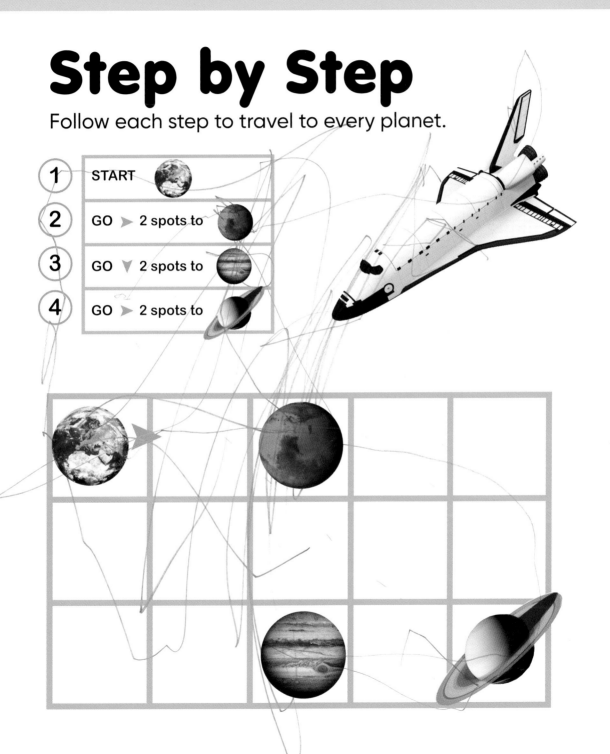

1	START
2	GO ▶ 2 spots to
3	GO ▼ 2 spots to
4	GO ▶ 2 spots to

Match It

Draw a line to connect each animal to its home.

Answers on page 115.

Spot the Shape

Circle this shape in the picture.

Odd One Out

Circle the object that does not belong.

Answers on page 115.

Do It!

Shake this book! Then turn the page.

What happened?

Answers on page 115.

Point

Point to the monkey's:

- Eyes
- Nose
- Tail
- Teeth

What Is Next?

What comes next in each pattern?

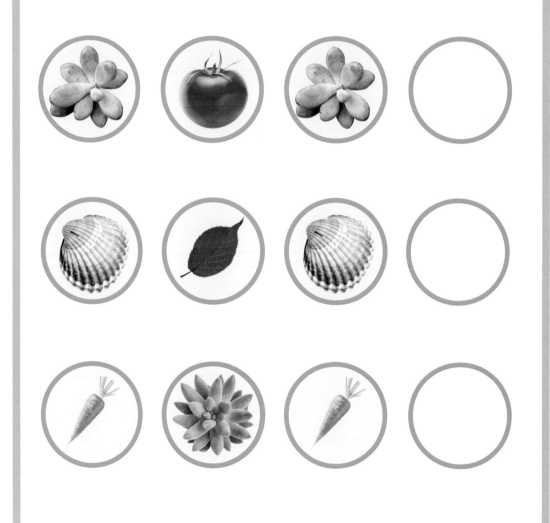

Answers on page 116.

Zoom In

Which animal matches the big picture?

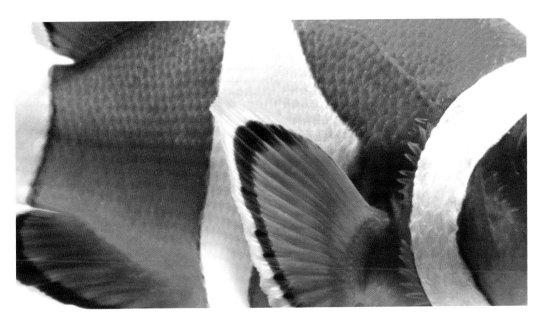

Two by Two

Draw a line to connect each butterfly with its twin.

Answers on page 116.

Find It

Circle these 3 fossils in the picture.

What Fits?

Which of these things would you bring to school?

Answers on page 117.

Draw It

Draw the missing parts.

- Draw 3 antennae

- Draw 1 arm

- Draw 1 foot

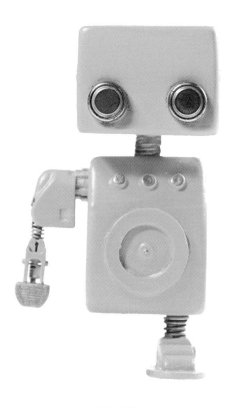

What Is Different?

Circle the 3 differences between these pictures.

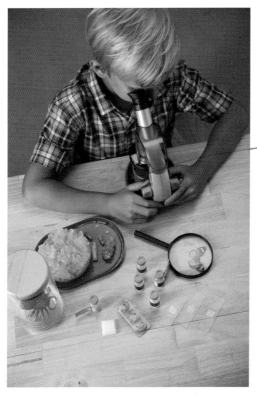
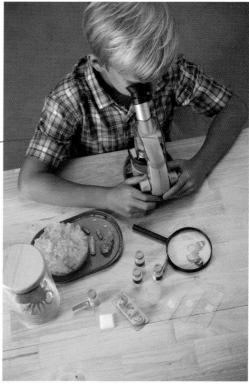

Answers on page 117.

Out of Order

These images are in the wrong order! What is the right order?

Hide and Seek

Circle the shell hiding among the tools and parts.

Answers on page 118.

Memory

Look at this picture for 1 minute. Remember it!
Then turn the page.

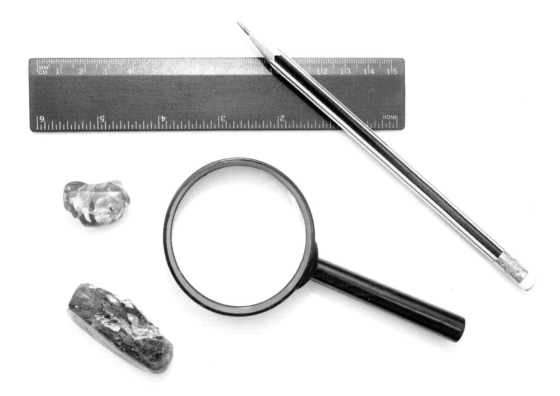

What is different here? Find 3 things that are different.

Answers on page 118..

Follow Me

Draw the path that goes through every feather.

START

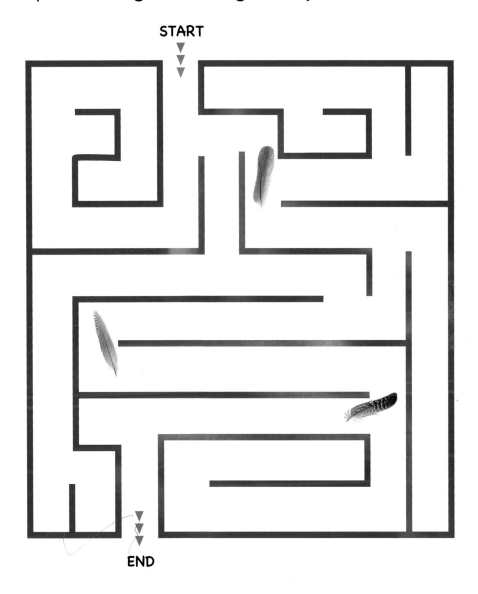

END

Step by Step

Follow each step to get the diver ready to find sharks.

(1)	START
(2)	GO ◀ 3 spots to
(3)	GO ▼ 2 spots to
(4)	GO ▶ 3 spots to

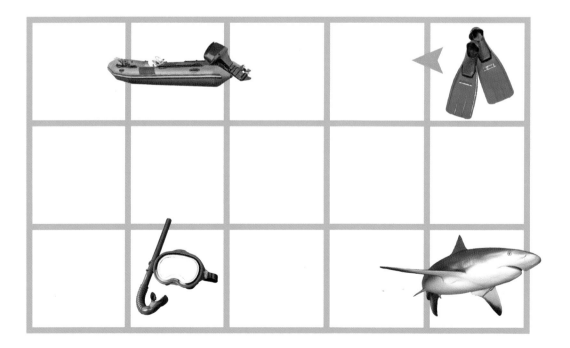

Answers on page 119.

Match It

Draw a line to connect each tool with what it is used for.

Spot the Shape

Find the U-shape inside the photo.

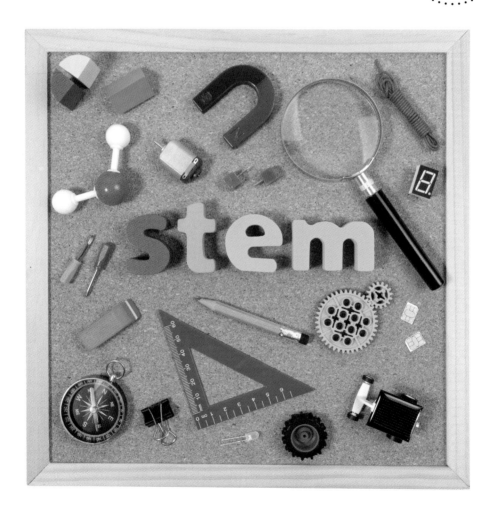

Answers on page 119.

Odd One Out

Circle the object that does not belong.

Point

Point to the crab's:

- Claws
- Legs
- Shell
- Eyes

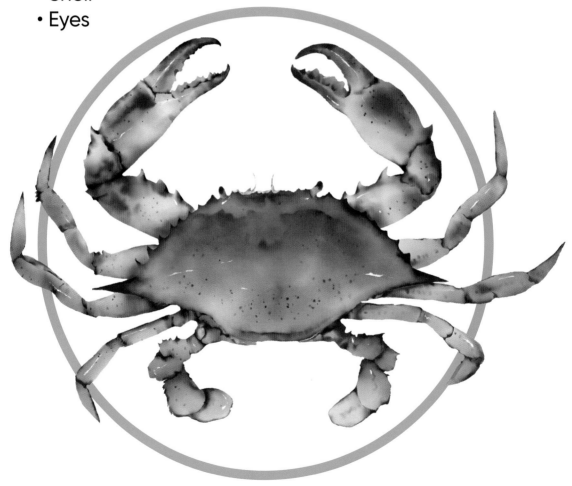

Answers on page 120.

Do It!

Blow on this book! Then turn the page.

What happened?

Answers on page 120.

What Is Next?

What comes next in each pattern?

Answers on page 120.

Zoom In

Which object matches the big picture?

Answers on page 120.

Two by Two

Draw a line to connect each tree with its twin.

Find It

Circle all the letters in the picture.

Answers on page 121.

What Fits?

Which of these are animals?

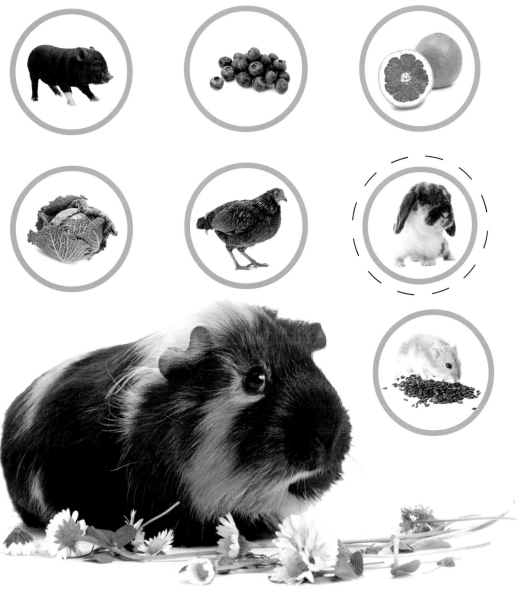

Answers on page 121.

Draw It

Draw the missing parts.

- Draw 1 bucket

- Draw 2 arms

- Draw 1 wheel

Answers on page 121.

What Is Different?

Circle the 3 differences between these two pictures.

Out of Order

These images are in the wrong order! What is the right order?

Answers on page 122.

Memory

Look at this picture for 1 minute. Remember it!
Then turn the page.

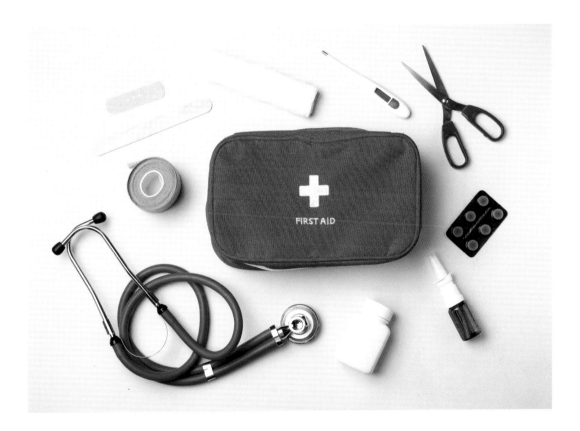

What is different here? Find 3 things that are different.

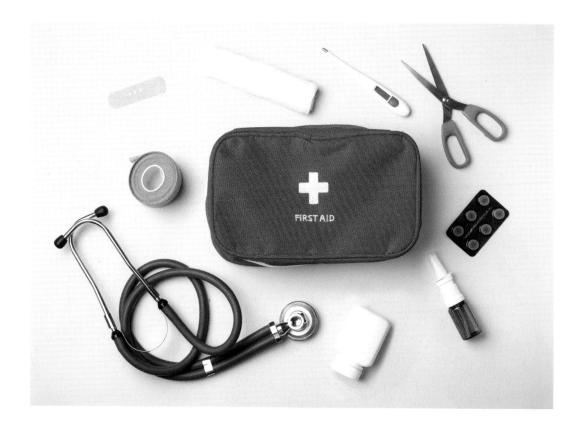

Answers on page 122.

Hide and Seek

Can you find these 4 different items?

Answers on page 122.

Follow Me

Draw the path that goes through every tool.

START

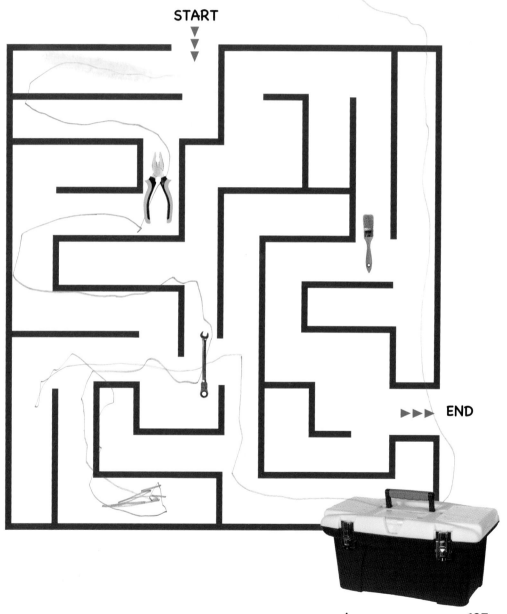

END

Answers on page 123.

Step by Step

Follow each step to get ready for school.

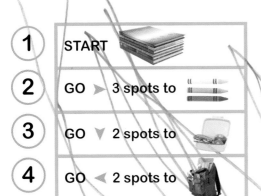

1	START
2	GO ▶ 3 spots to
3	GO ▼ 2 spots to
4	GO ◀ 2 spots to

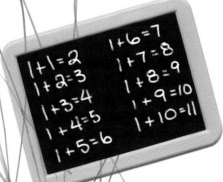

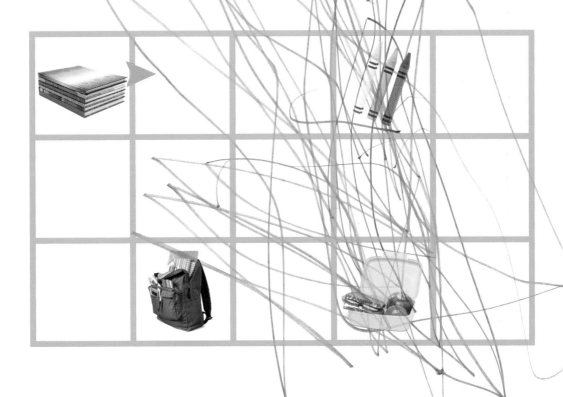

Answers on page 123.

Match It

Draw a line to connect each wheel to each vehicle.

Answers on page 123.

Spot the Shape

Find the 2 rectangles inside the photo.

Odd One Out

Circle the object that does not belong.

Answers on page 124.

Do It!

Shake this book! Then turn the page.

What happened?

Answers on page 124.

Point

Find the:

- Rider's helmet
- Rider's foot
- Rider's hand
- Motorcycle's wheels

Answers on page 124.

What Is Next?

What comes next in each pattern?

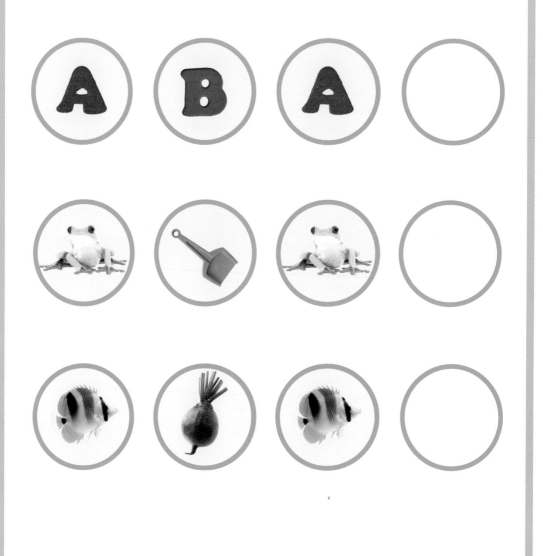

Answers on page 124.

Zoom In

Which object matches the big picture?

Two by Two

Draw a line to connect each dinosaur with its twin.

Answers on page 125.

Find It

Circle these 4 animals in the picture.

What Fits?

Which of these are letters?

Answers on page 125.

Draw It

Draw the missing parts.

- Draw 1 pot

- Draw 3 oranges

- Draw 3 leaves

What Is Different?

Circle the 3 differences between these pictures.

Answers on page 126.

Memory

Look at this picture for 1 minute. Remember it!
Then turn the page.

What is different here? Find 3 things that are different.

Answers on page 126.

Out of Order

These images are in the wrong order! What is the right order?

Answers on page 126.

Hide and Seek

Circle the apple hiding among the gears.

Answers on page 127.

Follow Me

Draw the path that goes through every flower.

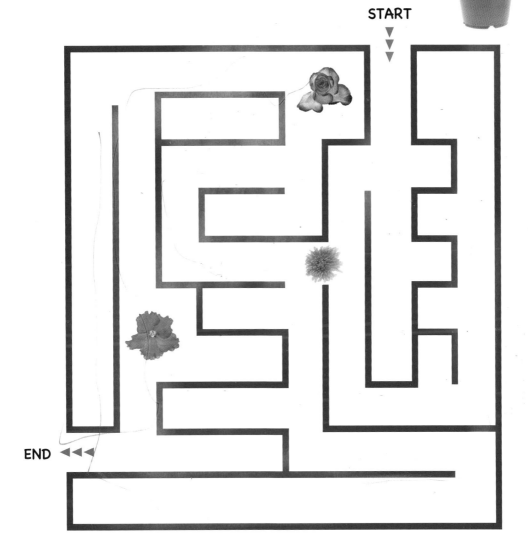

START

END ◄◄◄

Step by Step

Follow each step to go by all the machines at the construction site

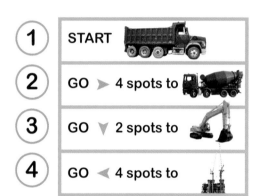

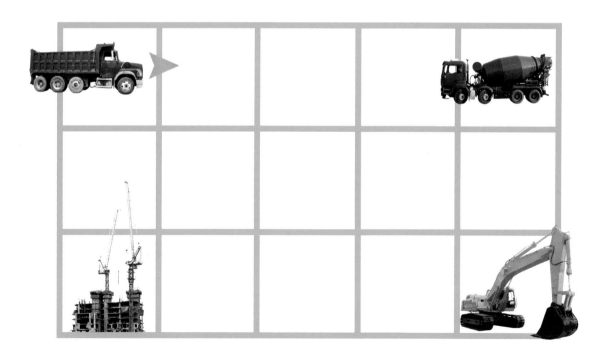

Answers on page 127.

Match It

Draw a line to connect each baby animal with its parent.

Spot the Shape

Find 4 half circles inside the photo.

Answers on page 128.

Point

Point to the penguin's:

- Beak
- Feet
- Belly
- Flippers

Follow Me: page 6

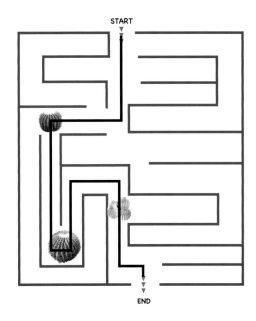

Match It: page 8

Step by Step: page 7

Spot the Shape: page 9

Odd One Out: page 10

Point: page 13

Do It!: pages 11–12
They jumped in the water.

What Is Next?: page 14

Zoom In: page 15

Find It: page 17

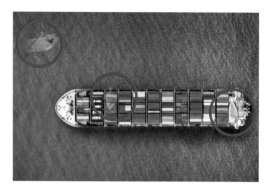

Two by Two: page 16

What Fits?: page 18

Draw It: page 19

Out of Order: page 21

What Is Different?: page 20

Hide and Seek: page 22

Memory: pages 23–24

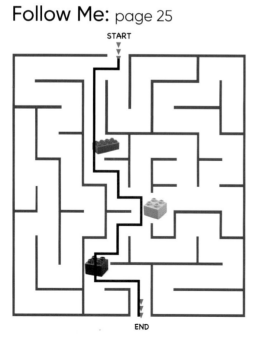

Step by Step: page 26

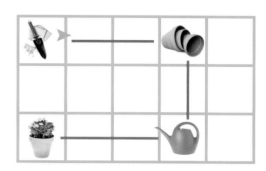

Match It: page 27

Follow Me: page 25

START

END

Spot the Shape: page 28

Point: page 30

Odd One Out: page 29

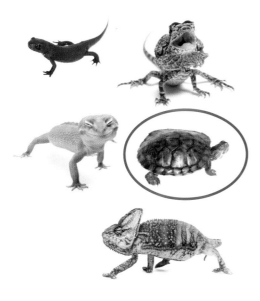

Do It!: pages 31–32
The dog rolled over.

Answers

What Is Next?: page 33

Two by Two: page 35

Zoom In: page 34

Find It: page 36

What Fits?: page 37

What Is Different?: page 39

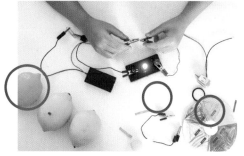

Draw It: page 38

Out of Order: page 40

Memory: pages 41–42

Hide and Seek: page 43

Follow Me: page 44

Step by Step: page 45

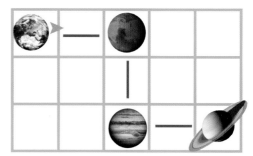

Match It: page 46

Odd One Out: page 48

Spot the Shape: page 47

Do It!: pages 49–50
The pine needles fell off.

Point: page 51

Zoom In: page 53

What Is Next?: page 52

Two by Two: page 54

Find It: page 55

Draw It: page 57

What Fits?: page 56

What Is Different?: page 58

Out of Order: page 59

Memory: pages 61–62

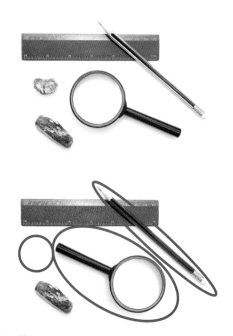

Hide and Seek: page 60

Follow Me: page 63

Step by Step: page 64

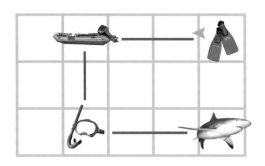

Spot the Shape: page 66

Match It: page 65

Odd One Out: page 67

Point: page 68

What Is Next?: page 71

Do It!: pages 69–70
The dandelion seeds blew away.

Zoom In: page 72

Two by Two: page 73

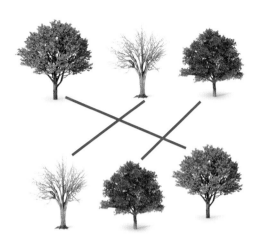

What Fits?: page 75

Find It: page 74

Draw It: page 76

What Is Different?: page 77

Memory: pages 79–80

Out of Order: page 78

Hide and Seek: page 81

Title: page 82

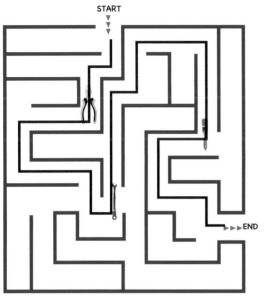

Match It: page 84

Step by Step: page 83

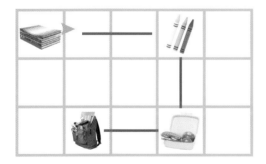

Spot the Shape: page 85

Odd One Out: page 86

Point: page 89

Do It! pages 87–88
The blocks fell.

What Is Next?: page 90

Answers

Zoom In: page 91

Find It: page 93

Two by Two: page 92

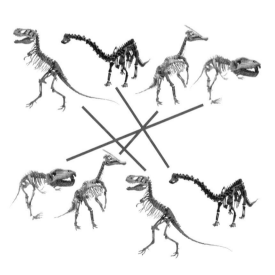

What Fits?: page 94

Draw It: page 95

Memory: pages 97–98

What Is Different?: page 96

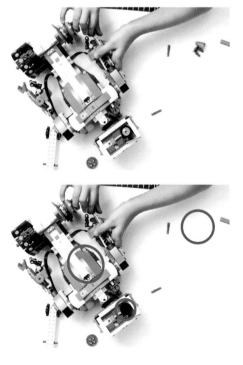

Out of Order: page 99

Hide And Seek : page 100

Step by Step: page 102

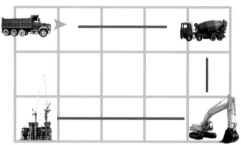

Follow Me: page 101

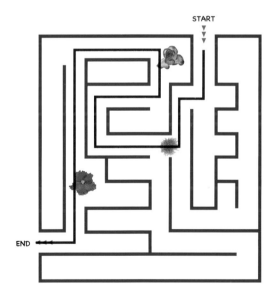

Match It: page 103

Spot the Shape: page 104

Point: page 105